THE DARK KNI ENIGMA

DECIPHERING THE CHARACTER, SYMBOLISM, PSYCHOLOGY, AND PHILOSOPHICAL FOUNDATIONS OF BATMAN

CREATED BY

ETERNIA PUBLISHING

ETERNIA
PUBLISHING

The Dark Knight Enigma: Deciphering The Character, Symbolism, Psychology, And Philosophical Foundations Of Batman
By Eternia Publishing and Zander Pearce

Author: Eternia Publishing and Zander Pearce
Contact: contact@eterniapublishing.com

ISBN: 9781312586284

CONTENT

INTRODUCTION

Batman, the iconic superhero of Gotham City, has captured the imagination of millions of people around the world since his creation in 1939. His dual identity as the billionaire Bruce Wayne and the vigilante Dark Knight has become a symbol of justice, courage, and heroism. But what lies beneath the cowl and cape of the Caped Crusader? What are the psychological motivations and symbolic meanings behind his character and actions? And how does his story relate to the great philosophical debates of our time?

In this book, we will embark on a journey of exploration into the world of Batman. We will decode the character symbolism and psychology that underpins his actions and delve into the complex philosophical theories that intersect with his story. In the following chapters, we will explore the following topics:

Throughout this book, we will delve into the rich and complex world of Batman, uncovering the psychology and philosophy that underpins the story of the Caped Crusader. By the end of this journey, readers will gain a deep understanding of the character, his motivations, and how his story relates to the great philosophical debates of our time.

THE DARK KNIGHT RISES: HISTORICAL CONTEXT AND CREATION OF BATMAN

The Dark Knight Rises is a 2012 superhero film that concludes Christopher Nolan's Batman trilogy. It is the third and final installment of the series, preceded by Batman Begins (2005) and The Dark Knight (2008). The film takes place eight years after the events of The Dark Knight, where the city of Gotham is threatened by the terrorist leader Bane.

The creation of Batman as a character dates back to 1939, where he was first introduced in Detective Comics #27. Bob Kane, along with writer Bill Finger, created Batman as a dark and brooding character with a tragic backstory. The character of Batman was intended to be a contrast to the brighter, more optimistic heroes of the time, such as Superman.

The character of Batman has continued to evolve over the years, with various writers and artists contributing to his mythology. One of the most notable interpretations of the character is Frank Miller's The Dark Knight Returns, a four-issue limited series published in 1986. Miller's take on Batman depicted him as an older, more jaded character, who had retired from crime-fighting only to return when Gotham was in need.

The historical context of The Dark Knight Rises is rooted in the aftermath of the September 11 attacks. The film was released in 2012, more than a decade after the attacks, but the influence of that event is evident throughout the movie. The character of Bane, a terrorist who seeks to destroy Gotham, can be seen as a reflection of the fears and anxieties of a post-9/11 world.

In creating The Dark Knight Rises, Christopher Nolan drew from a variety of sources, including the comic book storyline "Knightfall," which features the character of Bane breaking Batman's back. Nolan also drew from Charles Dickens' A Tale of Two Cities, which serves as a thematic inspiration for the film. The idea of a city divided between the wealthy and the poor, with revolution brewing beneath the surface, is a central theme of both the novel and the film.

The Dark Knight Rises serves as a fitting conclusion to Christopher Nolan's Batman trilogy, and a reflection of the fears and anxieties of a post-9/11 world. The character of Batman, created more than 80 years ago, continues to evolve and remain relevant to modern audiences.

THE BATMAN MYTHOS: SYMBOLISM AND ICONOGRAPHY OF THE CAPED CRUSADER

Batman is one of the most iconic and recognizable figures in popular culture, known for his brooding persona, advanced gadgets, and formidable physical prowess. Beyond these surface-level characteristics, however, lies a deeper layer of symbolism and iconography that has come to define the Batman mythos.

At its core, the Batman mythos is about justice and the struggle against corruption and evil. The character of Batman himself represents a symbol of hope and perseverance in the face of adversity. Bruce Wayne's decision to take on the mantle of Batman after witnessing the murder of his parents represents a refusal to accept the status quo, and a commitment to fighting against the injustices that plague Gotham City.

The iconic image of the bat serves as a visual representation of this commitment. Bats are often associated with fear and darkness, which reflects the way in which Batman is perceived by his enemies. However, the bat also represents a sense of primal power and primal fear, which Batman is able to harness to intimidate his opponents.

The costume worn by Batman also serves as an important symbol within the mythos. The black coloration and bat-like appearance of the costume are intended to inspire fear in his enemies, while the body armor and utility belt demonstrate his preparedness for any situation. The bat symbol on his chest serves as a beacon of hope for the citizens of Gotham, representing the idea that justice will prevail in the face of corruption and tyranny.

Another important aspect of the Batman mythos is the character's relationship with his rogues gallery of villains. Characters such as the Joker, the Riddler, and Two-Face are not just obstacles for Batman to overcome, but are also symbolic representations of different aspects of human nature. The Joker, for example, represents chaos and anarchy, while Two-Face represents the struggle between good and evil within the human psyche.

The Batman mythos is rich with symbolism and iconography that has come to define the character and his world. The bat symbol, the costume, and the rogues gallery all serve as important visual and thematic elements that reinforce the core themes of justice and the struggle against evil. The enduring popularity of the character speaks to the way in which these symbols and themes resonate with audiences of all ages and backgrounds.

THE PSYCHOLOGICAL PROFILE OF BATMAN: TRAUMA, GRIEF, AND REVENGE

Batman is one of the most complex and compelling characters in popular culture, known for his tragic backstory and intense focus on justice. At the heart of the character's psychology is a deep-seated trauma that has shaped his worldview and motivated his actions. This trauma, along with other psychological factors, has contributed to the development of Batman's unique personality and motivations.

The trauma that shaped Batman's psychology is the murder of his parents when he was a child. This event served as a catalyst for his obsession with justice and his decision to become a crime-fighter. The trauma also contributed to the development of his alter-ego, Bruce Wayne, who serves as a façade to mask the pain and trauma that Batman carries with him.

The grief that Batman experiences as a result of his parents' murder is another important aspect of his psychology. His grief is a driving force behind his actions, and serves as a reminder of the pain that he has endured. This grief is compounded by the fact that he was unable to save his parents, which has led him to become hyper-vigilant and to devote himself to a life of crime-fighting.

Revenge is another important psychological factor that motivates Batman. His desire for revenge is rooted in his trauma and grief, and drives him to seek justice against those who have wronged him or the citizens of Gotham City. His desire for revenge can be seen in his intense focus on apprehending criminals, and his willingness to use force to achieve his goals.

Finally, the character of Batman is also characterized by his vigilante behavior and his willingness to operate outside the law. This behavior is a direct result of his trauma, grief, and desire for revenge, and represents a refusal to accept the status quo. While Batman's actions may be questionable from a legal standpoint, they are seen as necessary by the character and by many of his fans.

The psychology of Batman is complex and multifaceted, shaped by his trauma, grief, and desire for revenge. These factors have contributed to the development of a unique personality and motivation, characterized by his obsession with justice and his willingness to operate outside the law. The enduring popularity of the character speaks to the way in which his psychology resonates with audiences of all ages and backgrounds.

THE BATMAN ARCHETYPE: AN ANALYSIS OF CARL JUNG'S SHADOW

The Batman archetype is a fascinating subject for analysis through the lens of Carl Jung's theory of the shadow. The shadow, according to Jung, is the part of the psyche that is composed of repressed or suppressed emotions, impulses, and desires that are considered unacceptable or incompatible with one's conscious self. The shadow is often represented by a dark, menacing figure that can be both frightening and alluring.

Batman, as a character, embodies many of the qualities associated with the shadow archetype. He is a vigilante who operates outside of the law, using force and intimidation to achieve his goals. He is often characterized as a brooding, dark figure who is motivated by a sense of justice, but who is also prone to violence and aggression.

The shadow archetype is often associated with the darker aspects of human nature, such as anger, aggression, and violence. Batman embodies these qualities, but he also represents a sense of control and discipline over these impulses. His training in martial arts and his use of advanced gadgets demonstrate his ability to channel his aggression in a focused and controlled manner.

The shadow archetype is also associated with the idea of the "other," or that which is different or alien to the conscious self. In this sense, Batman represents a kind of duality, as he is both Bruce Wayne and the Caped Crusader. His dual identity allows him to operate outside of society's norms and expectations, while also serving as a symbol of justice and hope.

Furthermore, the character of Batman can be seen as a symbol of transformation and rebirth. His decision to become Batman is a response to his trauma and grief, and represents a transformation from a helpless victim to a powerful and effective crime-fighter. This transformation is a central theme in Jungian psychology, which emphasizes the importance of confronting and integrating the shadow into the conscious self as a path to personal growth and individuation.

The Batman archetype is a rich subject for analysis through the lens of Carl Jung's theory of the shadow. The character embodies many of the qualities associated with the shadow archetype, including aggression, violence, and a sense of the "other." However, he also represents a sense of control and discipline over these impulses, as well as a symbol of transformation and personal growth. The enduring popularity of the character speaks to the way in which the Batman archetype resonates with audiences of all ages and backgrounds.

BATMAN AND ARISTOTLE: AN EXPLORATION OF THE CONCEPT OF VIRTUE ETHICS

The concept of virtue ethics, as espoused by Aristotle, is a philosophical framework that emphasizes the importance of cultivating good character and moral virtues in order to live a flourishing life. This framework is particularly relevant to the character of Batman, who embodies many of the virtues that Aristotle considered to be essential for a virtuous person.

One of the key virtues emphasized by Aristotle is courage, which he defined as the willingness to face danger and fear in order to do what is right. Batman exemplifies this virtue, as he frequently puts himself in harm's way in order to protect the citizens of Gotham City and uphold his sense of justice.

Another important virtue in Aristotle's philosophy is justice, which he defined as the virtue that enables individuals to act in accordance with what is fair and equitable. Batman's entire existence is built around the pursuit of justice, as he seeks to bring criminals to justice and protect the innocent.

Aristotle also emphasized the importance of practical wisdom, or the ability to make good decisions based on experience and knowledge. Batman's extensive training and expertise in martial arts, detective work, and technology demonstrate his practical wisdom, which he uses to effectively fight crime and protect Gotham City.

Furthermore, Aristotle stressed the importance of self-control, which he defined as the ability to regulate one's emotions and desires in order to act in accordance with reason. Batman's stoic demeanor and disciplined approach to crime-fighting exemplify this virtue, as he is able to channel his anger and grief into a focused and controlled pursuit of justice.

The concept of virtue ethics, as espoused by Aristotle, provides a useful framework for understanding the character of Batman. The virtues of courage, justice, practical wisdom, and self-control are all central to the character's persona and motivations. The enduring popularity of Batman as a cultural icon speaks to the way in which these virtues resonate with audiences of all ages and backgrounds, and highlight the timeless appeal of the concept of virtue ethics.

BATMAN AND STOICISM: INNER STRENGTH, SELF-CONTROL, AND STOIC PHILOSOPHY

The philosophy of stoicism is an ancient philosophical framework that emphasizes the cultivation of inner strength and self-control as a path to personal growth and happiness. The character of Batman embodies many of the key principles of stoicism, making it a useful lens for understanding his motivations and actions.

One of the core principles of stoicism is the idea of self-control, which involves regulating one's emotions and desires in order to act in accordance with reason. Batman embodies this virtue through his disciplined approach to crime-fighting, channeling his anger and grief into a focused and controlled pursuit of justice. His stoic demeanor and ability to maintain his composure in the face of danger are further evidence of his commitment to self-control.

Another important aspect of stoicism is the emphasis on inner strength, which involves developing a sense of resilience and the ability to withstand adversity.

Batman's tragic backstory and personal losses serve as a testament to his resilience and inner strength, as he is able to continue fighting for justice despite the many challenges and setbacks he faces.

Stoicism also emphasizes the importance of living in accordance with nature and the natural order of things. Batman's adherence to a personal code of ethics, as well as his commitment to upholding the law, can be seen as an expression of this principle. His actions are guided by a deep sense of purpose and a commitment to doing what is right, regardless of the personal cost.

Finally, the philosophy of stoicism emphasizes the importance of finding meaning and purpose in life. For Batman, his pursuit of justice and his commitment to protecting the citizens of Gotham City serve as a source of meaning and purpose, giving his life a sense of direction and significance.

The philosophy of stoicism provides a useful lens for understanding the character of Batman. The virtues of self-control, inner strength, living in accordance with nature, and finding meaning and purpose in life are all central to the character's motivations and actions. By embodying these principles, Batman serves as a powerful example of the enduring appeal of stoicism as a philosophy of personal growth and resilience.

BATMAN AND NIETZSCHE: THE WILL TO POWER AND THE ÜBERMENSCH

Friedrich Nietzsche's philosophy emphasizes the importance of the will to power as a fundamental drive for human action and creativity. The character of Batman embodies many of the key principles of Nietzsche's philosophy, particularly in his commitment to self-mastery and the pursuit of excellence.

The concept of the Übermensch, or the "superman," is also central to Nietzsche's philosophy. The Übermensch represents a kind of idealized human being who is able to transcend the limitations of conventional morality and social norms in order to achieve personal greatness. Batman's commitment to a personal code of ethics, as well as his willingness to operate outside of the law in pursuit of justice, can be seen as an expression of this concept.

Nietzsche also emphasized the importance of the will to power as a driving force for human creativity and achievement. Batman's extensive training and expertise in martial arts, detective work, and technology demonstrate his commitment to self-mastery and the pursuit of excellence.

His constant drive to improve his physical and mental abilities, as well as his dedication to using his skills to protect Gotham City, can be seen as an expression of the will to power.

Furthermore, Nietzsche's emphasis on individualism and self-expression can also be seen in Batman's character. Batman operates outside of conventional social norms and expectations, carving out his own path and pursuing his own sense of purpose. His commitment to using his skills and resources to make a difference in the world reflects the importance of individual agency and the pursuit of personal greatness.

The philosophy of Friedrich Nietzsche provides a useful framework for understanding the character of Batman. The concepts of the will to power and the Übermensch are central to Batman's motivations and actions, emphasizing his commitment to self-mastery and personal excellence. By embodying these principles, Batman serves as a powerful example of the enduring appeal of Nietzsche's philosophy as a framework for personal growth and individual greatness.

BATMAN AND UTILITARIANISM: ETHICS OF THE GREATER GOOD

Utilitarianism is a philosophical framework that emphasizes the importance of maximizing happiness and minimizing suffering in society. The character of Batman embodies many of the key principles of utilitarianism, particularly in his commitment to using his skills and resources to promote the greater good.

One of the core principles of utilitarianism is the importance of promoting the greatest amount of happiness for the greatest number of people. Batman's commitment to fighting crime and protecting the citizens of Gotham City can be seen as an expression of this principle. His actions are motivated by a desire to promote the well-being of others, even at the cost of his own personal safety and happiness.

Another important aspect of utilitarianism is the emphasis on minimizing suffering and promoting equality. Batman's commitment to social justice and his efforts to address the root causes of crime in Gotham City can be seen as expressions of this principle. By fighting against corruption and inequality, Batman is working to promote a more just and equitable society, thereby reducing suffering and promoting well-being for all.

Utilitarianism also emphasizes the importance of weighing the costs and benefits of different actions in order to maximize happiness and minimize suffering. Batman's use of violence and vigilantism can be seen as a form of calculated risk-taking, as he seeks to minimize harm while still achieving his goals. His use of advanced technology and strategic planning further reflect his commitment to maximizing the impact of his actions.

Finally, utilitarianism emphasizes the importance of empirical evidence and rational decision-making. Batman's reliance on detective work and forensic analysis, as well as his commitment to using data to inform his decision-making, reflect this principle. By basing his actions on evidence and reason, Batman is able to make more effective and efficient decisions, ultimately promoting the greater good.

The philosophy of utilitarianism provides a useful lens for understanding the character of Batman. His commitment to promoting the greater good, minimizing suffering, and maximizing happiness reflect many of the key principles of utilitarianism, making him a powerful symbol of the importance of ethical decision-making and social justice.

BATMAN AND DEONTOLOGY: MORAL DUTIES AND THE CATEGORICAL IMPERATIVE

Deontology is a moral philosophy that emphasizes the importance of following moral duties and principles, regardless of the consequences. The character of Batman embodies many of the key principles of deontology, particularly in his commitment to following a strict moral code and upholding justice.

One of the core principles of deontology is the idea that individuals have certain moral duties that must be followed, regardless of the consequences. Batman's strict adherence to his personal code of ethics, which includes a commitment to never kill or use excessive force, can be seen as an expression of this principle. His actions are motivated by a sense of duty to uphold justice and protect the innocent, rather than a desire for personal gain or satisfaction.

Another important aspect of deontology is the idea of the categorical imperative, which states that individuals should only act in ways that can be generalized to all other individuals in similar circumstances. Batman's commitment to treating all individuals fairly and impartially, regardless of their social status or personal relationships, can be seen as an expression of this principle.

He is committed to upholding justice and following his moral duties in a consistent and impartial manner.

Deontology also emphasizes the importance of respecting the autonomy and dignity of others. Batman's respect for the rule of law and his commitment to protecting individual rights and freedoms can be seen as expressions of this principle. He is committed to upholding the law and ensuring that justice is served in a fair and impartial manner.

Finally, deontology emphasizes the importance of rational decision-making and the use of reason in moral decision-making. Batman's reliance on careful planning, strategic thinking, and investigative work reflects this principle. By basing his actions on rational decision-making and moral duties, Batman is able to uphold justice and protect the innocent in a consistent and ethical manner.

The philosophy of deontology provides a useful framework for understanding the character of Batman. His commitment to moral duties and principles, the categorical imperative, respect for autonomy and dignity, and rational decision-making reflect many of the key principles of deontology, making him a powerful symbol of ethical decision-making and justice.

BATMAN AND VIRTUE ETHICS: THE IMPORTANCE OF MORAL CHARACTER

Virtue ethics is a moral philosophy that emphasizes the importance of developing moral character and virtues, rather than simply following rules or principles. The character of Batman embodies many of the key principles of virtue ethics, particularly in his commitment to developing a strong and virtuous moral character.

One of the core principles of virtue ethics is the idea that individuals should strive to develop virtuous moral character, rather than simply following rules or principles. Batman's commitment to developing his own moral character, including his strong sense of justice, determination, and courage, can be seen as an expression of this principle. He recognizes that being a hero is not just about following a set of rules, but also about embodying a set of virtues and values.

Another important aspect of virtue ethics is the idea that moral character is developed through habituation and practice. Batman's commitment to regular physical training, as well as his efforts to improve his detective and investigative skills, can be seen as an expression of this principle. He recognizes that developing virtuous moral character requires consistent practice and discipline.

Virtue ethics also emphasizes the importance of moral exemplars and role models in the development of moral character. Batman's commitment to following in the footsteps of his parents, who were killed by a criminal, and his efforts to protect the citizens of Gotham City, can be seen as an expression of this principle. He looks to his parents as a source of moral guidance and inspiration, and seeks to embody their values and virtues in his own actions.

Finally, virtue ethics emphasizes the importance of the individual's own judgment and reasoning in moral decision-making. Batman's commitment to using his own judgment and reasoning, rather than simply following the law or the rules of society, can be seen as an expression of this principle. He recognizes that being a hero requires making difficult moral decisions, and that these decisions must be based on personal judgment and reasoning.

The philosophy of virtue ethics provides a useful lens for understanding the character of Batman. His commitment to developing virtuous moral character, habituation and practice, moral exemplars and role models, and individual judgment and reasoning reflect many of the key principles of virtue ethics, making him a powerful symbol of the importance of ethical decision-making and moral character.

BATMAN
AND THE SOCIAL CONTRACT:
JUSTICE, FAIRNESS,
AND THE STATE OF NATURE

The social contract theory is a philosophical concept that explains the origin of society and the relationship between the individual and the state. In the case of Batman, his actions can be understood through the lens of social contract theory, particularly in his commitment to upholding justice, fairness, and the protection of the innocent.

One of the key principles of social contract theory is the idea that individuals come together to form a society and establish a government in order to protect themselves from the state of nature. The state of nature is a hypothetical scenario in which individuals live without any governing authority, leading to chaos and anarchy. Batman's commitment to protecting the citizens of Gotham City, particularly from the criminal element that threatens their safety and well-being, can be seen as an expression of this principle. He recognizes that without a system of justice and protection, the citizens of Gotham City would be vulnerable to the state of nature.

Another important aspect of social contract theory is the idea of justice and fairness. The social contract theory posits that individuals give up certain rights and freedoms in exchange for the protection and benefits of living in a society. In turn, the state is responsible for ensuring that justice is served fairly and impartially, and that the rights of the individual are protected.

Batman's commitment to upholding justice and fairness, particularly in his refusal to kill or use excessive force, can be seen as an expression of this principle. He recognizes that justice and fairness are essential for maintaining a functioning society, and that individuals must give up certain rights and freedoms in order to ensure these principles are upheld.

Finally, social contract theory emphasizes the importance of the consent of the governed. The state is only legitimate if it has the consent of the governed, and its actions must be consistent with the will of the people. Batman's actions can be seen as an expression of this principle, particularly in his efforts to protect the innocent and uphold justice in a way that reflects the values and desires of the citizens of Gotham City.

The philosophy of social contract theory provides a useful framework for understanding the character of Batman. His commitment to protecting the citizens of Gotham City from the state of nature, upholding justice and fairness, and respecting the consent of the governed reflect many of the key principles of social contract theory, making him a powerful symbol of the importance of ethical decision-making and the role of the state in protecting the rights and freedoms of its citizens.

BATMAN AND FEMINISM: GENDER ROLES AND REPRESENTATION IN THE DARK KNIGHT'S WORLD

Batman has been a cultural icon since his inception in 1939, but the representation of women in the Batman universe has been a subject of scrutiny and debate for decades. The feminist movement has long challenged gender stereotypes and advocated for equal representation in all aspects of society, including media and pop culture. In recent years, the Batman franchise has made some strides in terms of representation, but there is still much work to be done in terms of challenging traditional gender roles and stereotypes.

Historically, the representation of women in Batman media has been limited and often stereotypical. Female characters are frequently portrayed as love interests or damsels in distress, serving primarily as plot devices to advance the story of the male protagonist. This is evident in the character of Vicki Vale in the 1989 film "Batman" and Rachel Dawes in the 2005 film "Batman Begins." While both characters have agency and independence, they ultimately exist to serve the narrative arc of Batman.

In recent years, the Batman franchise has made efforts to provide more nuanced and complex representations of female characters. In the comic book series "Gotham City Sirens," female characters such as Harley Quinn and Catwoman are given their own stories and character development, independent of their relationships with male characters. Similarly, the 2019 film "Birds of Prey" centered on a team of female heroes and provided a more feminist perspective on the Batman universe.

Despite these positive developments, there is still much work to be done in terms of challenging traditional gender roles and stereotypes in the Batman universe. The franchise has a history of hyper-sexualizing female characters, particularly through costumes and poses that emphasize their bodies. Additionally, there is a notable lack of female representation behind the scenes, with few women serving as writers, directors, or producers.

While there have been positive developments in recent years, the Batman franchise still has a long way to go in terms of providing equitable and nuanced representation of women. By challenging traditional gender roles and stereotypes, and elevating the voices of female creators and characters, the Batman universe has the potential to become a more inclusive and feminist space.

BATMAN AND POSTMODERNISM: DECONSTRUCTION, AMBIGUITY, AND NARRATIVE IDENTITY

Postmodernism is a philosophical and cultural movement that challenges the idea of objective truth and the notion of a grand narrative. Instead, it focuses on individual experience and perception, and celebrates the plurality and ambiguity of meaning. The Batman franchise, with its complex characters, multi-layered narratives, and subversive themes, is a perfect example of postmodern storytelling.

One of the main characteristics of postmodernism is deconstruction, which involves breaking down traditional forms of storytelling and revealing the underlying power structures that shape our understanding of the world. The Batman franchise is a prime example of this, as it subverts traditional superhero tropes and presents a more complex and ambiguous vision of heroism. Batman, for example, is not a perfect hero, but a flawed and troubled individual who struggles with his own sense of morality and justice.

Another key feature of postmodernism is the idea of ambiguity, which rejects the notion of objective truth and embraces the idea of multiple and competing interpretations.

This is reflected in the Batman franchise through its complex and often contradictory narratives, which challenge the viewer to make their own sense of the story. For example, the character of the Joker, who is often portrayed as a chaotic and unpredictable force, embodies the postmodern idea of ambiguity and challenge to traditional notions of morality and order.

Narrative identity is also an important theme in postmodernism, as it highlights the way in which individuals construct their own sense of self through the stories they tell about themselves. The Batman franchise, with its focus on the psychological and emotional development of its characters, provides a rich and complex exploration of the construction of identity. This is particularly evident in the character of Batman, who creates his own identity through his transformation into a symbol of justice and order.

The Batman franchise embodies many of the key themes and characteristics of postmodernism, including deconstruction, ambiguity, and narrative identity. By subverting traditional forms of storytelling and challenging conventional notions of heroism, the franchise presents a complex and nuanced vision of the world that reflects the postmodern idea of plurality and diversity.

BATMAN AND PSYCHOANALYSIS: THE DARK KNIGHT'S PSYCHE, TRAUMA, AND DEFENSE MECHANISMS

Psychoanalysis is a psychological theory that emphasizes the importance of the unconscious mind, early childhood experiences, and defense mechanisms in shaping human behavior. The Batman franchise, with its focus on the psychological and emotional trauma of its characters, provides a rich and complex exploration of these themes.

One of the central concepts of psychoanalysis is the idea of the unconscious mind, which refers to the hidden parts of our psyche that influence our behavior without our awareness. In the case of Batman, his traumatic childhood experiences with the death of his parents and his subsequent transformation into a crime-fighter are central to his motivation and behavior. The unconscious influence of these experiences on Batman's psyche is a key theme in the franchise, as it highlights the importance of understanding the unconscious mind in shaping human behavior.

Another key theme in psychoanalysis is the idea of defense mechanisms, which are psychological strategies that individuals use to cope with the anxieties and stresses of everyday life. Batman's use of defense mechanisms, such as repression and projection, is evident in his character as he tries to cope with his traumatic past and the challenges of his current role as a crime-fighter. By exploring these defense mechanisms, the Batman franchise provides a nuanced understanding of the complex psychological makeup of its characters.

The idea of trauma is another important theme in psychoanalysis, and it is central to the character of Batman. His traumatic experiences with the death of his parents and the subsequent development of his alter-ego are key to his motivation and behavior. By exploring the impact of trauma on Batman's psyche, the franchise provides a powerful exploration of the psychological consequences of trauma, and the role it can play in shaping the behavior of individuals.

The Batman franchise provides a rich and complex exploration of the themes of psychoanalysis, including the unconscious mind, defense mechanisms, and trauma. By exploring the psychological makeup of its characters, the franchise provides a nuanced understanding of the complex interplay of the conscious and unconscious mind in shaping human behavior.

BATMAN AND NEUROSCIENCE: THE BRAIN AND SUPERHUMAN ABILITIES

The Batman franchise has always presented a character who has extraordinary abilities beyond what most humans are capable of. With its focus on the brain, neuroscience provides a valuable lens through which to explore the science behind Batman's abilities.

One of the central themes in neuroscience is the concept of neuroplasticity, which refers to the brain's ability to change and adapt throughout an individual's life. In the case of Batman, his intense training in martial arts, detective work, and technology has pushed the limits of what his brain is capable of, resulting in the development of superhuman abilities. By exploring the science behind neuroplasticity, the Batman franchise provides a realistic explanation for the character's extraordinary abilities, and highlights the potential of the human brain to achieve extraordinary feats.

Another key theme in neuroscience is the concept of neurodiversity, which refers to the natural variation in the way individuals' brains are wired.

The Batman franchise features a range of characters who display different neurological profiles, from the Joker's psychopathy to the Riddler's obsessive-compulsive tendencies. By exploring the science behind neurodiversity, the franchise provides a nuanced understanding of the complex interplay between brain function and behavior.

In addition, neuroscience provides insights into the mechanisms behind Batman's physical and cognitive abilities. For example, the use of neurotransmitters such as adrenaline and dopamine in the fight-or-flight response and the role of cognitive processes such as attention and memory in detective work. By exploring the science behind these processes, the franchise provides a scientific basis for the character's extraordinary abilities, highlighting the interplay between the brain and behavior.

The Batman franchise provides a rich and complex exploration of the themes of neuroscience, including neuroplasticity, neurodiversity, and the mechanisms behind extraordinary abilities. By exploring the science behind these concepts, the franchise provides a realistic and nuanced understanding of the complex interplay between the brain and behavior, and highlights the potential for humans to achieve extraordinary feats.

BATMAN AND TRANSHUMANISM: THE FUTURE OF HUMANITY AND TECHNOLOGICAL ADVANCEMENT

Batman, as a character, has always been associated with technology and the idea of using advanced tools and techniques to fight crime. This makes the concept of transhumanism particularly relevant to the Batman franchise, which explores the potential of technology to transform the human experience.

Transhumanism is a movement that seeks to use technology to enhance and extend human capabilities beyond the limits of biology. By using advanced technologies such as cybernetic implants, genetic engineering, and artificial intelligence, transhumanists hope to create a new era of humanity, in which individuals can live longer, healthier, and more fulfilling lives. Batman's use of technology, such as his gadgets and suit, is an example of transhumanism in action, as he is using advanced tools to enhance his physical and mental abilities.

The idea of transhumanism is particularly relevant in the context of the Batman franchise, as the stories often explore the limits of human potential, and the ways in which technology can be used to push those limits.

For example, Batman's suit is designed to enhance his strength, agility, and endurance, allowing him to fight crime with greater efficiency and effectiveness. Similarly, his Batcave is filled with advanced technology and equipment that enables him to gather and analyze information more effectively.

However, the Batman franchise also explores the potential dangers of transhumanism, particularly when it comes to the ethics of using advanced technologies to enhance human abilities. The character of Bane, for example, uses a drug called Venom to enhance his physical strength to the point of being superhuman, but at a great cost to his mental and physical health. The Joker, meanwhile, represents the dangers of unchecked technological advancement, using advanced weapons and gadgets to create chaos and destruction.

The Batman franchise provides a rich exploration of the themes of transhumanism, exploring the potential of technology to enhance and transform the human experience, while also highlighting the ethical concerns and potential dangers of unchecked technological advancement. As technology continues to advance, the Batman franchise will remain relevant as a means of exploring the complex relationship between humanity and technology.

BATMAN AND RELIGION: THE DARK KNIGHT'S MESSIANIC, CHRIST-LIKE SYMBOLISM

The character of Batman is often associated with religious symbolism and imagery, particularly with the concept of a messianic figure who is willing to sacrifice himself for the greater good. This is seen in the way that Batman is portrayed as a solitary figure, working alone to fight crime and protect the citizens of Gotham City, much like a prophet or messiah. Additionally, Batman's commitment to justice, fairness, and the greater good is reminiscent of the teachings of many religious traditions.

One of the most prominent examples of Batman's messianic symbolism is the way in which he is portrayed as a self-sacrificing hero, willing to give his own life to protect the citizens of Gotham City. This is seen in his willingness to face dangerous and powerful villains, such as the Joker, Bane, and Ra's al Ghul, without any concern for his own safety. In this way, Batman is seen as a Christ-like figure, willing to sacrifice himself for the greater good of humanity.

Another example of Batman's religious symbolism is the way in which he is portrayed as a solitary figure, working alone to fight crime and protect the citizens of Gotham City. This is reminiscent of the idea of a prophet or messiah, who works alone to spread a message of hope and salvation. Similarly, Batman is seen as a figure who is separate from society, working to protect it from the shadows.

Finally, Batman's commitment to justice, fairness, and the greater good is reminiscent of the teachings of many religious traditions, which emphasize the importance of treating others with compassion and respect. In this way, Batman is seen as a figure who is guided by a moral code, much like the teachings of many religious traditions.

The religious symbolism and imagery associated with the character of Batman is a testament to the enduring nature of the character and the complex themes that he embodies. As one of the most iconic and enduring superheroes in popular culture, Batman continues to provide a rich canvas for exploring complex ideas, including the idea of a self-sacrificing hero who is willing to fight for justice, fairness, and the greater good.

BATMAN AND POLITICAL PHILOSOPHY: THE FASCIST AND ANARCHIC ELEMENTS OF GOTHAM CITY

The city of Gotham in the Batman universe is often portrayed as a place of lawlessness and chaos, where traditional political institutions are unable to maintain order. This has led to many different interpretations of the political philosophy underlying the world of Batman, with some seeing it as a warning against the dangers of fascism, while others see it as a celebration of anarchism.

On the one hand, some see the portrayal of Batman as a vigilante who operates outside the law as a warning against the dangers of fascism. This interpretation suggests that Batman's actions are justified only because the traditional institutions of law and order have failed, and that his vigilantism is a response to a breakdown in society's ability to maintain order. This interpretation sees Batman as a sort of proto-fascist figure, one who is willing to use violence to maintain order, even if that means operating outside the law.

On the other hand, some see the portrayal of Batman as a hero who fights against the corruption and incompetence of traditional political institutions as a celebration of anarchism. This interpretation suggests that the world of Batman is one where the traditional political institutions have failed, and that only through direct action and personal responsibility can justice be achieved. This interpretation sees Batman as a figure who is willing to take matters into his own hands, and who operates outside the traditional political structures in order to achieve his goals.

The political philosophy of the Batman universe is complex and multifaceted, with many different interpretations and readings possible. While some see the world of Batman as a warning against the dangers of fascism, others see it as a celebration of anarchism. Ultimately, the world of Batman is one where traditional political institutions have failed, and where only through individual action and personal responsibility can justice be achieved.

BATMAN'S LEGACY: THE CAPED CRUSADER'S INFLUENCE ON POP CULTURE AND SOCIETY

Since his creation in 1939, Batman has become one of the most iconic characters in popular culture. The Caped Crusader has been the subject of countless comic books, TV shows, movies, video games, and merchandise, and has influenced generations of creators and fans. However, Batman's impact goes beyond the entertainment industry, as he has also had a significant influence on society and popular culture as a whole.

One of the ways that Batman has influenced pop culture and society is through his status as a cultural icon. Batman's logo, the Bat-Symbol, has become one of the most recognizable symbols in the world, and has been used in countless products and advertisements. This shows the cultural significance of the character, as he has become an instantly recognizable symbol of heroism and justice.

Another way that Batman has influenced pop culture and society is through his portrayal of complex moral dilemmas and psychological issues.

The character's traumatic past, his obsession with justice, and his struggle to maintain his own humanity while fighting crime have resonated with many readers and viewers. Batman's portrayal of complex psychological issues has inspired many creators to explore similar themes in their own work, and has helped to raise awareness of mental health issues.

Furthermore, Batman's legacy can also be seen in the countless characters that he has inspired. Characters like Nightwing, Batgirl, and Robin have all been influenced by Batman, and have gone on to become beloved characters in their own right. Additionally, Batman's rogues' gallery of villains, including the Joker, Catwoman, and Two-Face, has also become an integral part of the character's legacy, and has influenced many other creators to create their own memorable villains.

Batman's legacy is one of the most significant in pop culture and society. Through his status as a cultural icon, his portrayal of complex moral dilemmas and psychological issues, and his influence on other characters and creators, Batman has had a profound impact on popular culture and society as a whole. His enduring legacy is a testament to the enduring appeal of the character and his world.

BATMAN AND
THE PHILOSOPHY OF IDENTITY:
THE DUAL IDENTITY OF
BRUCE WAYNE
AND THE DARK KNIGHT

Batman's identity as both Bruce Wayne and the Dark Knight has been a defining characteristic of the character since his creation. This dual identity has been explored in many different ways, and has been the subject of much philosophical and psychological analysis.

One way that Batman's dual identity has been explored is through the concept of self-identity. Bruce Wayne's choice to become Batman is motivated by a desire to make a difference in the world and to right the wrongs that he has experienced. However, this decision also comes with a sacrifice, as Bruce must hide his true identity from the world in order to protect those he loves. This raises questions about the nature of identity and how much of it is defined by our external actions versus our internal desires and motivations.

Another aspect of Batman's dual identity is the idea of the divided self. Bruce Wayne and Batman represent different aspects of his personality, with Bruce representing the public face that he presents to the world and Batman representing his private, more primal instincts. This divide raises questions about the nature of the self and how much of it is defined by our conscious choices versus our unconscious desires.

Furthermore, Batman's dual identity can also be seen through the lens of ethics. Bruce Wayne's decision to become Batman is motivated by a desire to do good in the world, but he must also operate outside of the law in order to achieve his goals. This raises questions about the nature of morality and how much of it is defined by external rules versus internal motivations.

Batman's dual identity as Bruce Wayne and the Dark Knight has been the subject of much philosophical and psychological analysis. Through the concepts of self-identity, the divided self, and ethics, Batman's dual identity raises questions about the nature of the self and the nature of morality. The enduring popularity of the character is a testament to the enduring appeal of these themes and the rich, complex world that they create.

BATMAN AND EXISTENTIALISM: THE SEARCH FOR MEANING IN A CHAOTIC WORLD

Batman, one of the most iconic superheroes of all time, has captured the imaginations of fans for decades. From his brooding demeanor to his incredible physical prowess, there's something about Batman that speaks to the human condition. And when you look deeper, you can see that the Dark Knight is more than just a comic book character. In fact, Batman's journey is a perfect example of the philosophical concept of existentialism.

At its core, existentialism is a philosophical movement that emphasizes the individual's search for meaning and purpose in a chaotic and often absurd world. It focuses on the idea that humans are free beings who must create their own meaning in life, rather than relying on external factors such as religion or society. This concept is exemplified in the character of Batman, who, despite his incredible wealth and status, is plagued by a constant sense of emptiness and a lack of purpose.

Bruce Wayne, the man behind the mask, is driven by a deep desire to make a difference in the world. But his obsession with justice is rooted in a traumatic event from his childhood – the murder of his parents. This event shapes Bruce's entire worldview, leading him to believe that the world is inherently unjust and that it's his responsibility to set things right. This sense of purpose gives him the motivation to become Batman, but it also leads him down a dangerous path.

Throughout his many adventures, Batman confronts a variety of villains who embody different aspects of the absurd and chaotic nature of the world. The Joker, for example, represents the idea that life is inherently meaningless and that chaos is the only constant. This idea is particularly disturbing for Batman, who believes that there must be some kind of order to the universe. But in the face of the Joker's nihilism, Batman is forced to confront the fact that there may not be any inherent meaning in the world, and that he must create his own purpose.

This realization is central to the existentialist philosophy. In a world where there are no inherent values or meanings, it is up to each individual to create their own sense of purpose. For Batman, this means using his incredible skills and resources to fight crime and protect the people of Gotham City. But it also means accepting that he can never truly eliminate all the evil in the world, and that his quest for justice will always be ongoing.

One of the key themes of existentialism is the idea of authenticity – the idea that individuals must be true to themselves in order to find meaning in life. For Batman, this means embracing his dual identity as both Bruce Wayne and the Caped Crusader. By doing so, he is able to live a life that is true to his values and beliefs, even if it means sacrificing his own happiness and personal relationships.

Batman's journey is a perfect example of the existentialist philosophy. Through his quest for justice and his confrontations with the absurd and chaotic nature of the world, Batman is forced to confront the idea that there may not be any inherent meaning in life, and that he must create his own purpose. But through his commitment to his values and his sense of authenticity, Batman is able to find a sense of meaning and purpose in a world that often seems to lack both.

BATMAN AND UTILITARIANISM: BALANCING THE GREATER GOOD AND INDIVIDUAL RIGHTS

Batman, the iconic superhero of Gotham City, is known for his unwavering commitment to justice and his relentless pursuit of criminals. But beyond his superhero persona, Batman is also a complex character who raises important questions about the ethics of utilitarianism. Utilitarianism is a philosophical theory that holds that the best action is one that maximizes overall happiness or pleasure for the greatest number of people. In this essay, we will explore how Batman's actions reflect the tensions between the greater good and individual rights.

Batman is committed to protecting the people of Gotham City from the dangers that lurk within its streets. He uses his incredible wealth, intelligence, and physical abilities to fight crime, and he is not afraid to break the law to achieve his goals. This commitment to justice reflects a utilitarian perspective – Batman believes that the overall happiness of the citizens of Gotham City is more important than the individual rights of criminals.

However, Batman's actions often raise questions about the balance between the greater good and individual rights. For example, in "The Dark Knight," Batman is faced with the choice of whether to kill the Joker in order to prevent him from committing more heinous crimes. While this action may lead to the greater good by preventing the Joker from causing harm to innocent people, it violates the individual right to life.

Batman's commitment to utilitarianism is also evident in his use of surveillance technology. He uses a network of cameras and other devices to monitor the citizens of Gotham City, believing that this will help him to prevent crimes before they happen. While this strategy may be effective in reducing crime, it also raises important questions about individual privacy and civil liberties.

One of the key tensions in utilitarianism is the balance between the greater good and individual rights. Utilitarians argue that the best action is one that maximizes overall happiness or pleasure for the greatest number of people. However, this often comes at the expense of individual rights, which can be sacrificed for the greater good.

Batman's commitment to utilitarianism is not without its critics. Some argue that his actions violate the principles of justice and individual rights. Others argue that his tactics are too extreme and that they do more harm than good.

Ultimately, the tension between the greater good and individual rights is at the heart of Batman's actions. He is committed to protecting the citizens of Gotham City from harm, but he must also balance this commitment with the rights and freedoms of individual citizens. This tension reflects the broader ethical questions that we face in our own lives, as we seek to balance the greater good with the individual rights of those around us.

Batman's actions reflect the tensions between the greater good and individual rights. His commitment to utilitarianism is evident in his unwavering commitment to justice, but his tactics often raise important questions about the balance between the greater good and individual rights. While there may be no easy answers to these questions, Batman's journey highlights the ethical challenges that we face in our own lives as we seek to balance the needs of the many with the rights of the few.

BATMAN AND EUDAIMONIA: THE PURSUIT OF HUMAN FLOURISHING

Batman, the Dark Knight of Gotham City, is often portrayed as a brooding figure consumed by the pursuit of justice. However, beneath the surface lies a deeper theme that underlies his actions - the pursuit of eudaimonia, or human flourishing. In this essay, we will explore how Batman's quest for justice reflects his commitment to eudaimonia.

Eudaimonia is a philosophical concept that refers to human flourishing or the pursuit of the good life. It is a state of being in which a person is living in accordance with their true nature, and is characterized by happiness, fulfillment, and a sense of purpose. For Batman, the pursuit of eudaimonia is closely tied to his commitment to justice and his desire to protect the people of Gotham City.

Batman's commitment to justice reflects his belief that all people have the capacity to live a good life. He sees himself as a symbol of hope and a protector of the innocent, using his skills and resources to fight against injustice and bring criminals to justice. His pursuit of justice is not only a means to an end but is also an end in itself, reflecting his belief in the inherent value of living a just and righteous life.

Batman's commitment to eudaimonia is also evident in his relationships with others. He is a mentor to the young heroes in his universe, such as Robin and Batgirl, and he forms deep bonds with allies like Alfred and Commissioner Gordon. His relationships are characterized by loyalty, trust, and a sense of mutual support, reflecting his belief in the importance of human connection and community.

Furthermore, Batman's pursuit of eudaimonia is reflected in his commitment to personal growth and development. He is constantly seeking to improve himself, both physically and mentally, through rigorous training and self-reflection. His intense discipline and commitment to self-improvement reflect his belief that the pursuit of eudaimonia requires constant effort and self-reflection.

One of the key themes of eudaimonia is the importance of living in accordance with one's true nature. For Batman, this means embracing his identity as the Dark Knight of Gotham City and accepting the responsibility that comes with it. He is fully aware of the risks and dangers of his chosen path, but he accepts them willingly as part of his commitment to justice and his pursuit of eudaimonia.

Batman's pursuit of justice reflects his commitment to eudaimonia, or the pursuit of human flourishing. His belief in the inherent value of living a just and righteous life, his relationships with others, his commitment to personal growth and development, and his willingness to embrace his true nature all reflect his commitment to eudaimonia. As we consider the challenges and opportunities in our own lives, we can look to Batman as a model of the pursuit of eudaimonia, and a reminder of the importance of living in accordance with our true nature.

BATMAN AND KANTIAN ETHICS: THE MORAL IMPERATIVE OF DUTY AND REASON

Batman, the Caped Crusader, is a figure of justice and righteousness, whose actions are often guided by a strict moral code. This code is in line with Kantian ethics, a philosophical system that emphasizes the importance of duty and reason in guiding moral decision-making. In this essay, we will explore how Batman's actions and beliefs align with Kantian ethics.

Kantian ethics is centered around the concept of the moral imperative, which is the idea that moral decisions should be guided by a sense of duty and rationality, rather than personal desires or emotions. According to Kant, the moral worth of an action is determined by its adherence to a universal moral law, which is guided by reason and the categorical imperative.

Batman's actions are guided by a strict moral code that is in line with Kantian ethics. He operates within a set of guidelines that prioritize the safety and well-being of others, even at the expense of his own happiness or safety. This is reflected in his decision to become the Dark Knight of Gotham City, dedicating his life to fighting crime and protecting the innocent.

Batman's adherence to his moral code is also reflected in his interactions with others. He treats others with respect and dignity, even when they are his enemies, and he is committed to protecting the rights and freedoms of all people. He is willing to risk his own safety to ensure that justice is served, and he never wavers in his commitment to his principles.

Furthermore, Batman's actions are guided by reason and the categorical imperative, which is the idea that moral decisions should be made based on principles that can be applied universally, regardless of personal desires or preferences. This is reflected in Batman's refusal to kill his enemies, even when it would be easier or more expedient to do so. He believes that all life is sacred, and that taking a life would be a violation of the universal moral law.

Batman's commitment to reason is also evident in his interactions with his allies, such as Robin and Batgirl. He is committed to teaching them the skills and principles they need to become effective crime fighters, and he encourages them to think for themselves and make their own decisions. This reflects his belief in the importance of rationality and the use of reason in guiding moral decision-making.

Batman's actions and beliefs align with Kantian ethics, emphasizing the importance of duty and reason in guiding moral decision-making. His commitment to a strict moral code that prioritizes the safety and well-being of others, his interactions with others based on respect and dignity, and his adherence to universal principles that can be applied universally, all reflect his commitment to Kantian ethics. As we consider the challenges and opportunities in our own lives, we can look to Batman as a model of the importance of reason and duty in guiding our moral decision-making, and a reminder of the universal principles that guide our actions.

BATMAN AND MARXISM: CLASS STRUGGLE, SOCIAL INEQUALITY, AND POWER DYNAMICS

Batman, the Dark Knight of Gotham City, is a character who embodies themes of social justice, inequality, and power dynamics, making him a fitting subject for analysis through a Marxist lens. In this essay, we will explore how Batman's actions and beliefs relate to Marxist theory, specifically in regards to class struggle, social inequality, and power dynamics.

Marxism is a political and economic theory that emphasizes the struggle between different classes in society. According to Marx, society is divided into two primary classes: the ruling class, who own the means of production, and the working class, who labor to produce goods and services but do not own the means of production. This division creates a power dynamic that allows the ruling class to exploit the working class for their own benefit.

Batman's world is one of stark social inequality, where the wealthy and powerful control the city and the poor are left to struggle. Gotham is plagued by crime and corruption, with the city's wealthiest citizens often exploiting the poor for their own gain. This inequality and exploitation create a power dynamic that Batman seeks to disrupt.

Batman's actions often involve him fighting against the wealthy and powerful, who use their resources and influence to oppress and exploit the poor. For example, Batman's arch-nemesis, the Joker, often represents the forces of chaos and anarchy that arise in response to social inequality and injustice. In contrast, Batman represents the forces of order and justice, fighting to create a more equal and just society.

Furthermore, Batman's methods of fighting crime and injustice are in line with Marxist theory. He uses his wealth and resources to disrupt the power dynamic created by the ruling class, and he works to empower the working class by giving them the tools they need to fight back against oppression. Batman's allies, such as Robin and Batgirl, are often from working-class backgrounds, and he uses his influence to train and equip them to become effective crime fighters in their own right.

Batman's commitment to fighting social inequality is also evident in his interactions with the police. While he works closely with some police officers, he is also critical of the corruption and abuse of power that can arise within law enforcement. He recognizes that the police can be part of the power dynamic that creates social inequality and exploitation, and he works to disrupt that dynamic by holding corrupt officers accountable and working to build bridges between the police and the community.

Batman's actions and beliefs are consistent with Marxist theory, emphasizing the struggle between different classes in society, social inequality, and power dynamics. His fight against the wealthy and powerful, his use of resources to empower the working class, and his critical approach to law enforcement all reflect his commitment to creating a more equal and just society. As we continue to confront issues of social inequality and power dynamics in our own world, we can look to Batman as a model of resistance and justice.

BATMAN AND ABSURDISM: COPING WITH THE INHERENT MEANINGLESSNESS OF LIFE

Batman, the caped crusader of Gotham City, is a character who confronts the darker aspects of the human experience, including the inherent meaninglessness of life. His actions and beliefs can be analyzed through the lens of absurdism, a philosophy that emphasizes the lack of inherent meaning in the world and the individual's need to create their own purpose in life.

The Joker, one of Batman's most notorious enemies, represents the chaotic and meaningless aspects of life. He commits heinous crimes simply for the sake of causing chaos and destruction, embodying the idea that life has no inherent purpose or meaning. In contrast, Batman represents the individual's need to create their own meaning in the face of this meaninglessness.

Batman's tragic backstory, which involves the murder of his parents, provides a window into his struggle with the meaninglessness of life. After the death of his parents, Bruce Wayne dedicates his life to fighting crime in Gotham City, creating his own purpose and meaning in life through his role as the Dark Knight. His obsession with justice and his refusal to kill criminals reflect his belief in the importance of individual responsibility and the need to create meaning in the face of the absurdity of life.

Furthermore, Batman's actions are often motivated by his search for purpose and meaning. He fights against crime and corruption in Gotham City not only because it is the right thing to do, but also because it gives his life meaning and purpose. His dedication to his mission is unwavering, even in the face of adversity and danger, reflecting his belief that individuals must create their own meaning in life.

In addition, Batman's relationships with other characters in the Batman universe reflect his search for meaning. He takes on a mentor role with younger characters, such as Robin and Batgirl, providing them with guidance and training to become effective crime fighters. His relationships with other heroes, such as Superman and Wonder Woman, reflect his desire for connection and belonging in a world that can often feel meaningless and chaotic.

The absurdity of life is also reflected in Batman's villains. Characters like the Riddler, who revel in meaningless puzzles and games, and Two-Face, whose coin flips determine his actions, embody the idea that life is random and without inherent purpose. Batman's ability to outsmart and defeat these villains reflects his belief in the importance of individual agency and the power of human will in the face of the meaningless of life.

Batman's actions and beliefs reflect the philosophical ideas of absurdism, emphasizing the lack of inherent meaning in the world and the individual's need to create their own purpose in life. His dedication to fighting crime and corruption in Gotham City, his relationships with other characters, and his ability to outsmart and defeat his villains all reflect his belief in the importance of individual responsibility and agency in the face of the absurdity of life. As we confront the meaninglessness of life in our own world, we can look to Batman as a model of resilience and determination in the face of adversity.

BATMAN AND NIETZSCHEAN NIHILISM: THE DEATH OF GOD AND THE WILL TO POWER

Friedrich Nietzsche's philosophy of nihilism emphasizes the rejection of traditional values and beliefs, including the belief in God and the idea of objective meaning in life. Batman's character can be examined through the lens of Nietzschean nihilism, as he also challenges traditional values and beliefs in his fight against crime and corruption in Gotham City.

In Nietzsche's philosophy, the "death of God" refers to the rejection of traditional religious beliefs and values, which he saw as restricting individual freedom and creativity. Batman, like Nietzsche, rejects traditional values and beliefs, instead creating his own moral code based on his personal beliefs and experiences.

Batman's character reflects Nietzsche's idea of the "will to power," which emphasizes the individual's desire for control and dominance. Batman's obsession with justice and his need to bring criminals to justice reflect his desire for power and control over his environment. He also possesses a strong sense of self-will and determination, reflecting Nietzsche's idea of the individual's ability to overcome obstacles through their own strength of will.

Moreover, Batman's belief in the importance of individual responsibility and agency reflects Nietzsche's idea of the "superman," an individual who possesses exceptional qualities and has the ability to shape their own destiny. Batman's determination to fight crime and corruption in Gotham City reflects his belief that he can make a difference in the world through his own actions and strength of character.

Batman's relationships with other characters in the Batman universe reflect his rejection of traditional values and beliefs. His relationship with Commissioner Gordon, who is often conflicted about Batman's vigilante tactics, reflects Batman's rejection of traditional law enforcement methods. Similarly, his relationship with Robin reflects his rejection of traditional family structures and his desire to create his own sense of belonging and connection.

Batman's villains, who represent chaos and destruction in Gotham City, also reflect Nietzsche's idea of the rejection of traditional values and beliefs. Characters like the Joker and Two-Face represent the absence of objective meaning in life, as they engage in senseless violence and destruction without any apparent motivation or purpose.

However, Batman's character differs from Nietzsche's nihilism in one important way. While Nietzsche believed that the rejection of traditional values and beliefs would lead to the creation of new values and a new meaning in life, Batman's character does not offer a clear solution to the problem of nihilism. Rather, his actions reflect a constant struggle to create meaning and purpose in a world that seems devoid of it.

Batman's character can be analyzed through the lens of Nietzschean nihilism, reflecting his rejection of traditional values and beliefs and his emphasis on the individual's will to power and agency. While his actions reflect a struggle to create meaning and purpose in the face of nihilism, his dedication to fighting crime and corruption in Gotham City reflects his belief in the importance of individual responsibility and strength of character. As we confront the challenges of nihilism in our own lives, we can look to Batman as a model of resilience and determination in the face of the absence of objective meaning.

BATMAN AND POSTMODERNISM: DECONSTRUCTION, AMBIGUITY, AND NARRATIVE IDENTITY

Postmodernism is a philosophical movement that emphasizes the rejection of absolute truths and objective reality, and instead emphasizes the importance of language, discourse, and individual interpretation. Batman's character can be examined through the lens of postmodernism, as his story and identity are shaped by a complex web of language, narrative, and interpretation.

One of the key tenets of postmodernism is deconstruction, or the analysis of the underlying assumptions and power structures in language and discourse. Batman's story and identity are constructed through a variety of narratives, including comic books, movies, and television shows. Each of these narratives offers a different interpretation of Batman's character, reflecting the postmodern idea that meaning is always shifting and contingent on context.

Furthermore, Batman's character is characterized by ambiguity and complexity. He is neither purely good nor purely evil, but instead operates in a moral gray area. This reflects the postmodern idea that there are no clear-cut categories or absolutes, and that meaning is always open to interpretation.

The concept of narrative identity is also central to postmodernism. Batman's identity is shaped by the stories and myths that surround him, as well as his own personal history and experiences. This reflects the postmodern idea that identity is not fixed or essential, but is instead a product of the stories we tell about ourselves and the world around us.

Moreover, Batman's relationship with his villains reflects the postmodern idea of the construction of identity through opposition. Batman's identity is defined in opposition to the chaos and destruction represented by his villains, and his actions are a constant struggle to maintain order and control in a world that is inherently unstable and uncertain.

Batman's identity is also shaped by his relationships with other characters in the Batman universe. His relationship with Robin, for example, reflects the postmodern idea of the fragmentation and multiplicity of identity. Robin represents a different aspect of Batman's identity, and their relationship is constantly shifting and evolving.

Finally, Batman's character reflects the postmodern idea of the rejection of objective reality and the importance of individual interpretation. Each person who encounters Batman's story and character will interpret it in their own way, and there is no single "correct" interpretation. This reflects the postmodern idea that meaning is always subjective and contingent on individual perspective.

Batman's character can be analyzed through the lens of postmodernism, reflecting the importance of language, narrative, and interpretation in the construction of identity and meaning. Batman's story is characterized by ambiguity, complexity, and opposition, reflecting the postmodern rejection of absolute truths and objective reality. As we navigate the complexities of postmodernism in our own lives, we can look to Batman as a model of resilience and adaptability in the face of constant change and uncertainty.

BATMAN AND ENVIRONMENTAL ETHICS: THE RESPONSIBILITY TO PROTECT THE NATURAL WORLD

Environmental ethics is a branch of philosophy that explores the ethical responsibilities of human beings towards the natural world. Batman's character can be examined through the lens of environmental ethics, as his actions reflect a sense of responsibility towards the protection and preservation of the natural world.

One of the key tenets of environmental ethics is the belief in the intrinsic value of nature, which means that nature has value in and of itself, regardless of its usefulness to human beings. Batman's character embodies this belief, as he frequently intervenes in situations where the natural world is threatened, even when it does not directly impact human beings.

Batman's commitment to environmental protection can be seen in his role as a protector of Gotham City. In many stories, Gotham is portrayed as a polluted and decaying urban environment, where the natural world is often neglected and forgotten. Batman's efforts to clean up the city and restore its natural spaces reflect a sense of responsibility towards the environment, and a belief in the importance of preserving nature for its own sake.

Furthermore, Batman's relationship with the Batcave, his secret underground lair, reflects his connection to the natural world. The Batcave is filled with natural wonders, including stalactites, underground lakes, and a variety of flora and fauna. Batman's decision to locate his base of operations within the natural world reflects his respect for the environment and his belief in the importance of protecting it.

Batman's character also reflects the importance of sustainability and conservation. In many stories, Batman uses advanced technology to develop eco-friendly solutions to environmental problems. For example, he installs solar panels on the Batcave to generate clean energy, and develops advanced filtration systems to purify Gotham's polluted rivers.

Moreover, Batman's relationship with animals reflects a sense of responsibility towards the natural world. He is often depicted as having a close bond with bats, which he sees as fellow creatures of the night. This reflects a belief in the interconnectedness of all living things, and a sense of responsibility towards protecting and preserving the natural world.

Finally, Batman's character reflects the importance of environmental justice. Environmental justice is the idea that all people, regardless of their race, class, or socioeconomic status, have a right to a healthy and safe environment. Batman's actions often involve protecting the natural world from those who would exploit it for profit, reflecting a commitment to environmental justice and the belief that all people deserve access to clean air, water, and natural resources.

Batman's character can be analyzed through the lens of environmental ethics, reflecting his commitment to protecting and preserving the natural world. His actions reflect a belief in the intrinsic value of nature, the importance of sustainability and conservation, and a sense of responsibility towards environmental justice. As we navigate the complexities of environmental ethics in our own lives, we can look to Batman as a model of environmental responsibility and a reminder of the importance of protecting and preserving the natural world for future generations.

BATMAN AND EPISTEMOLOGY: THE LIMITS OF KNOWLEDGE AND THE NATURE OF TRUTH

Epistemology is a branch of philosophy that deals with the nature of knowledge, belief, and truth. Batman's character can be analyzed through the lens of epistemology, as his actions and beliefs reflect a skepticism towards traditional sources of knowledge and an interest in seeking out the truth.

One of the key themes of epistemology is the problem of skepticism, which is the idea that our knowledge of the world is uncertain and subject to doubt. Batman's character embodies this idea, as he is often portrayed as a skeptical and mistrustful figure who is constantly questioning the information he receives. This is particularly evident in his relationship with the police and the media, both of which he often views with suspicion and skepticism.

Furthermore, Batman's character reflects a skepticism towards traditional sources of knowledge, such as academia and institutionalized forms of authority. Instead, he relies on his own experiences and intuition to guide his actions, reflecting a belief in the importance of personal knowledge and individual inquiry.

Another key theme of epistemology is the nature of truth, and the various theories that attempt to define it. Batman's character embodies a form of correspondence theory, which holds that truth is the agreement between a proposition and the reality it describes. This is reflected in his dedication to uncovering the truth behind various mysteries and conspiracies, and his belief in the importance of objective evidence and logical deduction.

However, Batman's character also reflects a recognition of the limits of knowledge and the subjectivity of truth. He is often depicted as grappling with the unknowability of certain aspects of the world, and the limitations of human understanding. This is particularly evident in his relationship with the Joker, a character who represents chaos and irrationality, and whose actions defy logical explanation.

Finally, Batman's character reflects a commitment to the pursuit of knowledge and the importance of intellectual curiosity. He is often depicted as a highly intelligent and analytical figure who is constantly seeking out new information and learning from his experiences. This reflects a belief in the importance of ongoing inquiry and the value of knowledge for its own sake.

Batman's character can be analyzed through the lens of epistemology, reflecting his skepticism towards traditional sources of knowledge, his commitment to uncovering the truth, and his recognition of the limits of knowledge and the subjectivity of truth. As we navigate the complexities of epistemology in our own lives, we can look to Batman as a model of intellectual curiosity and a reminder of the importance of questioning our assumptions and seeking out new knowledge.

BATMAN AND ONTOLOGY: THE NATURE OF BEING AND EXISTENCE

Ontology is a branch of philosophy that deals with the nature of being and existence. It is concerned with questions about what exists, what can be said to exist, and how things are related to each other. Batman's character can be analyzed through the lens of ontology, as his actions and beliefs reflect a complex understanding of the nature of being and existence.

One of the key themes of ontology is the nature of identity, and how individuals understand themselves in relation to the world around them. Batman's character reflects a complex understanding of identity, as he grapples with questions about his own sense of self and his relationship to Gotham City. His identity as Batman is closely tied to his sense of duty and responsibility, and reflects a belief in the importance of using one's abilities to make a positive impact on the world.

Another key theme of ontology is the nature of reality, and how individuals understand the world around them. Batman's character embodies a form of realism, which holds that there is a world that exists independently of human perception or interpretation.

This is reflected in his dedication to uncovering the truth behind various mysteries and conspiracies, and his belief in the importance of objective evidence and logical deduction.

Furthermore, Batman's character reflects a belief in the importance of personal agency and free will. He is often depicted as a figure who is able to shape his own destiny through his actions, reflecting a belief in the power of individual choice and the ability to shape one's own reality.

Finally, Batman's character reflects a recognition of the interconnectedness of all things, and the importance of understanding the relationships between individuals and the broader systems they exist within. This is reflected in his commitment to protecting Gotham City from various threats, and his recognition of the importance of addressing systemic issues such as crime and corruption.

Batman's character can be analyzed through the lens of ontology, reflecting his complex understanding of identity, reality, agency, and interconnectedness. As we grapple with questions about the nature of being and existence in our own lives, we can look to Batman as a model of how to navigate these complex philosophical concepts with integrity, dedication, and a commitment to making the world a better place.

BATMAN AND AESTHETICS: THE ROLE OF ART AND BEAUTY IN HUMAN EXPERIENCE

Aesthetics is the branch of philosophy concerned with the study of beauty, art, and taste. As a character, Batman can be analyzed through the lens of aesthetics, as his actions and the world he inhabits are deeply tied to questions about the role of art and beauty in human experience.

One way in which aesthetics is relevant to Batman is through the visual aesthetic of the character and his world. Batman's iconic costume, along with the dark and gritty aesthetic of Gotham City, are both integral to the character's identity and the world he inhabits. This visual aesthetic reflects a broader interest in the role of visual art and design in human experience, as well as the way in which aesthetics can shape our perceptions of the world around us.

Another way in which aesthetics is relevant to Batman is through the role of narrative and storytelling in human experience. Batman is a character who has been told and retold in countless different forms over the years, reflecting a deep interest in the power of storytelling and the importance of narrative in shaping our understanding of the world. This interest in narrative is reflected in the various adaptations of Batman across different media, as well as the way in which the character's origin story and various story arcs have been retold and reimagined over the years.

Furthermore, Batman's commitment to justice and righteousness can be seen as reflective of a broader interest in the role of morality and ethics in human experience. The aesthetic appeal of Batman's character is tied to his status as a symbol of justice and the triumph of good over evil, reflecting a belief in the power of moral ideals and ethical principles to shape our understanding of the world and our place within it.

Finally, the character of Batman is also relevant to aesthetics in his role as a cultural icon and symbol of popular culture. The popularity of Batman reflects a broader interest in the role of popular culture and mass media in shaping our understanding of the world and our place within it. The character's popularity has also given rise to various fan communities and subcultures, reflecting a broader interest in the role of culture and subcultural identities in shaping our experiences of the world.

The character of Batman is deeply tied to questions about the role of art and beauty in human experience. Whether through his visual aesthetic, his commitment to justice and righteousness, or his role as a cultural icon, Batman reflects a complex understanding of the power of aesthetics to shape our perceptions of the world and our place within it. As we grapple with questions about the role of art and beauty in our own lives, we can look to Batman as a model of how these concepts can be used to create meaning and value in the world around us.

BATMAN AND SOCIAL PSYCHOLOGY: GROUP DYNAMICS AND INTERPERSONAL RELATIONSHIPS

Batman is a character that provides a rich source of material for exploring concepts in social psychology, particularly in relation to group dynamics and interpersonal relationships.

One of the key areas of social psychology that is relevant to Batman is the study of group dynamics. Throughout his various stories and adaptations, Batman is often depicted as working alongside a team of allies, such as Robin, Batgirl, and various members of the Justice League. These group dynamics provide a fertile ground for exploring questions about leadership, communication, and cooperation within groups.

For example, the dynamic between Batman and Robin can be seen as reflecting broader questions about the nature of mentorship and hierarchical relationships within groups.

Similarly, the dynamics between Batman and other members of the Justice League, such as Superman or Wonder Woman, can be seen as reflecting broader questions about teamwork and the role of individual strengths and weaknesses within a group.

Furthermore, Batman's relationships with his enemies, particularly the Joker, provide a rich source of material for exploring questions about interpersonal relationships and social influence.

For example, the relationship between Batman and the Joker can be seen as reflecting broader questions about the role of power dynamics and social influence in shaping our relationships with others. Similarly, the various other villains that Batman encounters provide an opportunity to explore questions about the role of social norms and group identity in shaping our behaviors and attitudes towards others.

Finally, Batman's role as a vigilante and protector of Gotham City can be seen as reflecting broader questions about the nature of social responsibility and the role of social norms and values in shaping our behaviors towards others. The character's commitment to justice and righteousness reflects a belief in the importance of social norms and values in guiding our actions and behaviors towards others, while his struggles against the corrupt systems of power in Gotham City provide a rich source of material for exploring questions about social inequality and the role of social change in promoting justice and fairness in society.

The character of Batman provides a rich source of material for exploring concepts in social psychology, particularly in relation to group dynamics and interpersonal relationships. Whether through his relationships with his allies and enemies, his role as a protector of Gotham City, or his struggles against systems of power and social inequality, Batman reflects a complex understanding of the role of social norms, values, and beliefs in shaping our behaviors and attitudes towards others. As we grapple with questions about the nature of human relationships and social dynamics, we can look to Batman as a model of how these concepts can be explored and understood in the context of popular culture.

BATMAN AND BEHAVIORAL PSYCHOLOGY: LEARNING, CONDITIONING, AND BEHAVIOR MODIFICATION

Batman, the iconic DC Comics character, has a rich history that provides ample material for exploring concepts in behavioral psychology. Throughout his stories, adaptations, and interactions with other characters, Batman displays various behaviors that can be analyzed through the lens of behavioral psychology, including learning, conditioning, and behavior modification.

One key concept in behavioral psychology is learning, or the process by which we acquire new information or skills. Batman is often depicted as a highly skilled and capable crime-fighter, but this proficiency did not come naturally. Through his training with various mentors, such as Ra's al Ghul and the League of Assassins, Batman was able to acquire a wide range of skills, including martial arts, detective work, and tactical planning. His ability to learn and apply new skills is a testament to the power of deliberate practice and focused learning, key concepts in behavioral psychology.

Another key concept in behavioral psychology is conditioning, or the process by which our behaviors are shaped through association with stimuli. One example of conditioning in the world of Batman is the relationship between Batman and the Bat-Signal. Whenever the signal is projected in the sky, Batman responds, even if he is in the middle of a different task. This response is conditioned through repeated exposure to the signal and its association with the need for Batman's assistance. Other examples of conditioning can be seen in Batman's relationships with his allies and enemies, as well as in his use of various gadgets and tools.

Behavior modification, or the process of changing behavior through reinforcement or punishment, is another key concept in behavioral psychology that can be applied to Batman. One example of behavior modification in the world of Batman is Batman's treatment of his enemies. In some adaptations, Batman is shown as willing to use violence and force to stop his enemies, while in others he is shown as more willing to negotiate and find nonviolent solutions. This difference in approach can be seen as reflecting broader questions about the role of punishment and reinforcement in shaping behavior.

Finally, the use of operant conditioning in Batman's training of his various sidekicks, such as Robin and Batgirl, provides a rich source of material for exploring concepts in behavioral psychology. By providing rewards for desirable behaviors and punishment for undesirable behaviors, Batman is able to shape the behavior of his allies and encourage them to become more effective crime-fighters. However, this approach also raises questions about the ethical implications of using behavior modification techniques to shape the behavior of others.

The world of Batman provides a rich source of material for exploring concepts in behavioral psychology, including learning, conditioning, and behavior modification. Through his interactions with other characters, his use of gadgets and tools, and his training of his allies, Batman provides numerous examples of how behavior can be shaped and modified through reinforcement, punishment, and association with stimuli. As we continue to study the nature of behavior and its influence on our lives, we can look to the world of Batman as a model for exploring and understanding these concepts in the context of popular culture.

BATMAN AND EVOLUTIONARY PSYCHOLOGY: THE BIOLOGICAL BASIS OF HUMAN BEHAVIOR

Evolutionary psychology is the study of the biological basis of human behavior, and how our evolutionary history has shaped the way we think, feel, and behave. The world of Batman provides a fascinating lens through which to explore these concepts, as the characters and their behaviors are deeply rooted in the evolutionary history of the human species.

One key concept in evolutionary psychology is adaptation, or the process by which organisms change in response to their environment. Batman is an example of an organism that has adapted to a hostile and dangerous environment, specifically the city of Gotham. Through his training, his gadgets, and his tactics, Batman has developed a range of adaptive strategies that enable him to survive and thrive in this environment. These strategies include physical prowess, analytical thinking, and strategic planning, all of which have been honed through years of training and experience.

Another key concept in evolutionary psychology is natural selection, or the process by which certain traits become more common in a population due to their advantages in survival and reproduction. In the world of Batman, we can see examples of natural selection at work in the characters and their behaviors. For example, the villains that Batman faces are often depicted as having extreme and maladaptive behaviors, such as the Joker's sadistic tendencies or Two-Face's pathological indecision. These behaviors may have been advantageous in the past, but in the modern world they are no longer adaptive, and the characters suffer as a result.

One area of particular interest in the world of Batman is the psychology of fear. Fear is a powerful emotion that has evolved as a way of keeping organisms safe from danger. In the world of Batman, fear is a central theme, as the character uses fear as a tool to intimidate his enemies and gain the upper hand in fights. This strategy is effective because it taps into deep-seated evolutionary fears that are hard-wired into the human brain, such as the fear of darkness, the fear of predators, and the fear of violence.

Finally, the world of Batman provides a rich source of material for exploring the relationship between biology and social behavior. One example of this is the relationship between Batman and his allies, such as Robin and Batgirl. These relationships are based on a complex mix of biological and social factors, including trust, loyalty, and a shared sense of purpose. By exploring these factors in the context of evolutionary psychology, we can gain a deeper understanding of how social bonds are formed and maintained, and how they contribute to our survival and well-being.

The world of Batman provides a fascinating lens through which to explore the concepts of evolutionary psychology. By examining the characters and their behaviors in the context of our evolutionary history, we can gain a deeper understanding of how our biology shapes our thoughts, feelings, and behaviors. Through its exploration of adaptation, natural selection, fear, and social behavior, the world of Batman provides a rich source of material for exploring the biological basis of human behavior, and the ways in which we have evolved to survive and thrive in a complex and challenging world.

BATMAN AND HUMANISM: THE VALUE OF HUMAN AGENCY AND DIGNITY

Humanism is a philosophical and ethical perspective that emphasizes the value and agency of human beings, individually and collectively. It is concerned with the well-being and flourishing of human beings, as well as their potential to achieve their goals and realize their full potential. In the world of Batman, we can see the principles of humanism at work in the character of Bruce Wayne, and in the way he interacts with the world around him.

One of the core principles of humanism is the belief in human agency, or the ability of individuals to make choices and take actions that shape their lives and the world around them. Bruce Wayne is a prime example of human agency in action, as he uses his wealth, intelligence, and physical prowess to take on the mantle of Batman and fight crime in Gotham City. He is driven by a deep sense of responsibility and a desire to make the world a better place, and he is willing to take risks and make sacrifices to achieve his goals.

Another key principle of humanism is the belief in human dignity, or the inherent worth and value of each individual. This principle is reflected in the way that Batman treats his enemies, even those who have committed heinous crimes. While he is firm in his commitment to justice and the rule of law, he also recognizes the humanity of those he fights against, and he strives to treat them with respect and compassion. This is evident in his interactions with villains such as the Joker, whom he recognizes as a complex and troubled individual, rather than a one-dimensional caricature.

A third principle of humanism is the belief in the potential of human beings to achieve their goals and realize their full potential. This is reflected in the way that Batman mentors and trains his allies, such as Robin and Batgirl. He recognizes their potential as individuals, and he works to help them develop their skills and abilities so that they can contribute to the fight against crime in their own way. This is also reflected in the way that Batman approaches his own training and development, constantly pushing himself to improve and refine his skills so that he can be the best possible version of himself.

Finally, the principles of humanism are reflected in the way that Batman approaches his relationships with others, both individually and collectively. He recognizes the value of interpersonal connections, and he works to build and maintain strong relationships with his allies, such as Alfred and Commissioner Gordon. He also recognizes the importance of collective action, and he works with other heroes and organizations to address larger issues of social justice and inequality in Gotham City.

The world of Batman provides a rich source of material for exploring the principles of humanism, including the value of human agency, dignity, potential, and social connection. Through the character of Bruce Wayne and his interactions with the world around him, we can gain a deeper understanding of the ways in which these principles shape our lives and our relationships with others. By emphasizing the value and potential of human beings, and by recognizing the interconnectedness of all human beings, the world of Batman provides a powerful message of hope and inspiration, and a reminder of the importance of working together to build a better world.

BATMAN AND VIRTUE EPISTEMOLOGY: THE IMPORTANCE OF INTELLECTUAL VIRTUES

Virtue epistemology is a branch of epistemology that focuses on the role of intellectual virtues in knowledge acquisition and evaluation. Intellectual virtues are character traits or dispositions that enable individuals to acquire and assess knowledge effectively and responsibly. In the world of Batman, we can see the importance of intellectual virtues in the character of Bruce Wayne/Batman and the way he approaches his role as a crime-fighter and detective.

One of the key intellectual virtues emphasized in virtue epistemology is curiosity. Curiosity is the desire to learn and explore new ideas, and it is a critical component of knowledge acquisition. In the world of Batman, we see the importance of curiosity in the way that Bruce Wayne approaches his role as a detective. He is constantly asking questions and seeking out information in order to solve crimes and bring justice to Gotham City. He is also deeply curious about the world around him, and he spends a great deal of time studying and learning about a wide range of subjects, from science and technology to criminology and psychology.

Another important intellectual virtue is open-mindedness. Open-mindedness is the willingness to consider new ideas and evidence, even if they challenge one's existing beliefs. This is critical for knowledge acquisition and evaluation, as it enables individuals to avoid confirmation bias and be more objective in their assessments. In the world of Batman, we see the importance of open-mindedness in the way that Bruce Wayne approaches his investigations. He is willing to consider a wide range of theories and possibilities, even those that might seem unlikely or unconventional. This enables him to approach his investigations with a fresh perspective and avoid being limited by his preconceptions.

A third important intellectual virtue is intellectual humility. Intellectual humility is the recognition that one's own knowledge and understanding is limited, and that there is always more to learn. This is critical for knowledge acquisition and evaluation, as it enables individuals to be more receptive to new ideas and evidence, and to avoid being overconfident in their own abilities. In the world of Batman, we see the importance of intellectual humility in the way that Bruce Wayne approaches his role as a detective and crime-fighter. He recognizes that he does not have all the answers, and he is constantly seeking out new information and perspectives to broaden his understanding of the world.

Finally, the virtue of intellectual courage is also emphasized in virtue epistemology. Intellectual courage is the willingness to pursue knowledge and truth, even in the face of obstacles or opposition. This is critical for knowledge acquisition and evaluation, as it enables individuals to be persistent in their pursuit of knowledge, and to stand up for what they believe in, even in the face of adversity. In the world of Batman, we see the importance of intellectual courage in the way that Bruce Wayne approaches his role as a crime-fighter. He is willing to take on powerful foes and stand up for what he believes is right, even in the face of danger or opposition.

The world of Batman provides a rich source of material for exploring the principles of virtue epistemology, including the importance of intellectual virtues such as curiosity, open-mindedness, intellectual humility, and intellectual courage. Through the character of Bruce Wayne/Batman and his approach to knowledge acquisition and evaluation, we can gain a deeper understanding of the ways in which intellectual virtues shape our understanding of the world and our ability to navigate complex issues. By emphasizing the importance of these virtues, the world of Batman provides a powerful message about the value of knowledge and the importance of approaching the world with an open and curious mind.

BATMAN AND BIOETHICS: ETHICAL DILEMMAS IN BIOTECHNOLOGY AND MEDICINE

Batman, as a superhero, has to deal with various ethical issues that arise due to the use of biotechnology and medical advancements. These advancements offer new opportunities and challenges, which require ethical considerations. Bioethics, a branch of ethics that deals with the moral dilemmas related to biotechnology and medical research, provides a framework to address such issues.

One of the most significant ethical dilemmas that arise from the use of biotechnology and medical advancements is the question of whether it is right to use them to enhance human abilities. Batman himself is an example of this, as he is a human who has used technology and training to enhance his physical abilities beyond human limits. The ethical implications of this are complex. Some argue that using such enhancements could lead to unequal distribution of resources, as only a few could afford to access them. Others argue that the use of such enhancements is inherently unfair, as it leads to an uneven playing field.

Another issue that arises in bioethics is the use of technology and medical advancements to prolong life. Batman's character has often dealt with this issue, as he tries to protect Gotham City from villains who seek to harm its citizens. The question arises whether it is ethical to prolong life at all costs, even if it means sacrificing quality of life. This is a difficult question, as it requires balancing the desire to save lives with the need to preserve the dignity and autonomy of individuals.

Batman's alter ego, Bruce Wayne, is also a philanthropist who invests in medical research to improve people's lives. However, this also raises ethical questions related to the use of resources. The question arises whether it is ethical to invest in medical research when there are pressing social issues that require attention. This is particularly relevant in the context of Gotham City, which is plagued by crime and social inequality.

One of the most controversial issues in bioethics is the use of embryonic stem cells for medical research. Stem cells have the potential to cure a wide range of diseases, but their use raises ethical questions, as they are harvested from human embryos. This raises questions about the ethics of using embryos for research purposes and the dignity and autonomy of the embryo. Batman, as a defender of justice and autonomy, would be expected to have a strong opinion on this issue.

Another issue in bioethics is the use of genetic engineering to alter the traits of humans. This raises ethical concerns related to the ethics of playing with nature and the implications of such alterations for future generations. This is a complex issue, as it requires balancing the desire to enhance the abilities of humans with the need to preserve the autonomy and dignity of individuals.

Batman's character deals with various ethical issues related to the use of biotechnology and medical advancements. These issues require ethical considerations, which are provided by the field of bioethics. The use of biotechnology and medical advancements offers new opportunities and challenges, which require careful ethical considerations. The issues that arise in bioethics, such as the use of technology to enhance human abilities, the use of medical advancements to prolong life, and the use of genetic engineering to alter the traits of humans, require careful ethical considerations and balancing of the desire to save lives with the need to preserve dignity and autonomy.

BATMAN AND CYBER ETHICS: ETHICAL CONSIDERATIONS IN THE DIGITAL AGE

The rise of technology has given birth to an era of digital interconnectedness that has transformed the way we interact, work, and live. The internet and its associated technologies have brought about significant changes to various aspects of human life, including business, education, social life, entertainment, and healthcare. While these developments have brought about numerous benefits, they have also raised ethical concerns and challenges. As a character who relies heavily on technology and innovation to combat crime, Batman is a fitting subject to explore the intersection of ethics and technology in the digital age.

One of the primary concerns in cyber ethics is the issue of privacy. In the digital age, the amount of personal data that is collected, processed, and stored is vast, and the risk of data breaches and identity theft is high. Batman, as a vigilante who operates outside of the law, must tread carefully in this area. The use of surveillance technologies to monitor Gotham's criminal underworld raises questions about privacy and the limits of surveillance. Batman must balance his need for information with the privacy rights of the citizens of Gotham.

Another area of cyber ethics that is relevant to Batman is cybersecurity. The use of technology by Batman and his allies makes them vulnerable to cyber attacks by criminals and other malicious actors. The risk of cybercrime and the potential damage it can cause to Gotham's infrastructure and critical systems is significant. Batman must consider the ethical implications of his use of technology and ensure that the systems he uses are secure and not easily hacked.

In addition to privacy and cybersecurity, there are ethical considerations around the use of artificial intelligence and autonomous systems. Batman's arsenal of tools includes advanced technologies such as the Batcomputer and the Batmobile, which incorporate artificial intelligence and autonomous systems. The use of these technologies raises questions about the role of human agency and the potential consequences of relying on machines to make decisions. Batman must ensure that these systems are programmed to act in the best interests of society and that their use does not compromise human dignity or autonomy.

Another area of concern in cyber ethics is the digital divide, which refers to the unequal distribution of access to digital technologies and information. While Batman and his allies have access to cutting-edge technologies, the citizens of Gotham who lack access to technology are at a disadvantage.

The digital divide can exacerbate existing social and economic inequalities and can lead to exclusion and marginalization. Batman must consider the impact of technology on society and work to ensure that access to technology is more equitable.

Finally, the issue of accountability is critical in cyber ethics. Batman operates outside of the law and has no formal accountability mechanisms. His actions are often justified by his desire to protect Gotham and its citizens. However, this lack of accountability raises ethical concerns around the use of vigilantism to achieve justice. Batman must consider the impact of his actions on society and work to ensure that his actions are justified and do not undermine the rule of law.

The digital age has brought about significant changes to human life, and with it, ethical challenges and considerations. As a character who relies heavily on technology and innovation, Batman must navigate these challenges and consider the ethical implications of his actions. From privacy to cybersecurity, artificial intelligence to the digital divide, and accountability, Batman's use of technology must be guided by ethical principles that ensure the protection of human dignity, agency, and justice.

BATMAN AND EDUCATION: THE ROLE OF LEARNING AND KNOWLEDGE IN HUMAN DEVELOPMENT

Batman's commitment to lifelong learning and personal growth is one of his defining characteristics. Throughout his crime-fighting career, he has constantly sought to improve his skills and knowledge, not only in martial arts and detective work but also in a variety of academic fields. Batman's dedication to education reflects the importance of learning and knowledge in human development.

One aspect of education that Batman exemplifies is the value of self-directed learning. While Batman has received formal education from prestigious universities such as Princeton and Cambridge, he also recognizes the importance of learning through personal exploration and experimentation. He is constantly experimenting with new gadgets and techniques, seeking to improve his abilities and stay ahead of the curve. This approach to learning emphasizes the importance of creativity, curiosity, and innovation in the learning process.

Batman's interest in a wide range of academic fields also demonstrates the value of interdisciplinary learning. He has demonstrated knowledge of biology, chemistry, physics, engineering, psychology, and many other fields. His ability to integrate these diverse areas of knowledge allows him to approach problems from multiple perspectives and develop more effective solutions. This approach to education emphasizes the importance of broadening one's intellectual horizons and seeking out knowledge from a variety of sources.

Another aspect of education that Batman values is the importance of mentorship and collaboration. While he is often portrayed as a solitary figure, Batman has worked with a number of partners and mentors throughout his career, including Robin, Batgirl, and Alfred. He recognizes that no one person can possess all the knowledge and skills necessary to tackle the complex problems he faces, and he seeks out the guidance and support of others when necessary. This approach to education emphasizes the importance of social learning and the value of relationships in the learning process.

Batman's commitment to education also reflects the importance of continuous learning and personal growth. Despite his many successes, Batman is never complacent and is always seeking to improve his abilities and knowledge. He recognizes that learning is a lifelong process and that there is always more to discover and understand. This approach to education emphasizes the importance of self-reflection and a growth mindset in the learning process.

Finally, Batman's dedication to education highlights the importance of education in promoting social justice and equity. He recognizes that access to education and knowledge is not evenly distributed in society and works to provide educational opportunities to those who have been historically marginalized or underserved. This approach to education emphasizes the importance of education as a tool for promoting social mobility and creating more just and equitable societies.

Batman's commitment to education highlights the importance of self-directed learning, interdisciplinary learning, mentorship and collaboration, continuous learning and personal growth, and education as a tool for promoting social justice and equity. These principles of education are essential for promoting lifelong learning and personal development and are key to creating a more just and equitable society.

ABOUT ETERNIA PUBLISHING

This guide is a result of thorough research from various official sources, including books, courses, biographies, and interviews by renowned experts in the respective fields.

The content is presented in a simplified and practical manner, leaving out redundancies, unnecessary and irrelevant information, and only focusing on the key concepts.

The sources of knowledge are carefully selected and relevant, and the guide aims to provide a broad overview of the reader's topics of interest.

The ultimate goal is to ensure that the text is easily understandable, practical, and pleasant to read.

The reader can acquire a large amount of knowledge from more than one reliable source, making it a useful resource.

The guide is designed to help readers learn and understand specialized information with the greatest effectiveness.

COPYRIGHT

LEGAL DISCLAIMER

This book aims to provide information and entertainment to its readers. The author has used reliable sources for the content, but cannot guarantee its accuracy or validity and is not responsible for any errors or omissions.

The book is not intended to be professional advice and should not replace the guidance of experts. The reader should consult professionals before using any protocols or medical treatments described in the book.

The reader agrees to use the information in the book at their own risk and the author is not liable for any costs, expenses, damages, or professional fees that may arise from using the information in the book. This disclaimer applies to any direct or indirect use of the information, and the author is not liable for any damages, negligence, criminal intent or other causes of action.

REVIEWS

We hope that this book has been helpful in providing a deeper understanding and analysis of the subject.

We appreciate your time in reading and hope that you found the content useful.

If you enjoyed the book, we would be grateful if you could leave a positive review, as this is one of the ways for new authors like us to gain visibility and improve the quality of our writing.

Thank you for your support!

The Dark Knight Enigma: Deciphering The Character, Symbolism, Psychology, And Philosophical Foundations Of Batman
By Eternia Publishing and Zander Pearce

Author: Eternia Publishing and Zander Pearce
Contact: contact@eterniapublishing.com

ISBN: 9781312586284

Printed in Great Britain
by Amazon

32926366R00077